Nature Opens the Door

Poems inspired by Forest Bathing walks

"As you sit on a hillside, or lie prone under the trees of the forest, or sprawl wet-legged by a mountain stream, the great door, that does not look like a door, opens."
—Stephen Graham

CAROL MARCY

For Cynthia Spencer Marcy

ISBN: 979-8-218-96679-9

Front cover image: Getty Images
Artwork within the book: Carol Marcy
Book design: Paraclete Design

First printing edition 2023

Contents

Preface

The magic of poetry

Nature opens the door, singing to the heart, inviting us to experience a deep sense of connection and belonging. In the words of Chief Seattle in 1854, "The earth does not belong to us: we belong to the earth...All things are connected like the blood that unites one family...We did not weave the web of life; we are merely a strand on it."

If you were on a Forest Bathing walk with me, I would tell you that my secret agenda is that you will come to experience yourself as an integral part of the forest, not separate from it. It is my hope that these poems will do the same by weaving you with words into an awareness of your participation in the intricate, intimate vast web of life, belonging to something so beautiful and amazing. The forest has a lot to teach us about how to live well and foster a community of connection.

Come walk with me with awareness along the song-lines of the heart. Breathe deep belly breaths. Feel the diaphragm invite air into your lungs, pushing gently on the organs in your belly giving them a sweet massage. Feel the soles of your feet come into conversation with the Earth. Experience the warmth of the sunlight tangling with your hair. Bathe in the light in and around you, opening and energizing your heart. Enjoy!!

A Forest Bathing Walk meditation experience

I enter the forest. Gradually, breath flushes distractions, bringing with it a heart centered focus. Opening my heart to the surrounding beauty, I call out to Nature and her hand maidens, the nature spirits of this place. "I come to you in peace and beauty, opening and inviting connection, in gratitude to the glory of creation here, to the living being of the forest." Mindfully, I feel my feet connecting with the Earth underneath my weight. The temperature and texture of that foot felt embrace, gliding, balancing, connecting through movement. I feel my knees follow suit, bending, allowing a steadiness of gait. Hips join in with a swinging movement. The breath rises up from my belly, freeing my spine to respond to the subtle dance of purposefully walking forward. As the breath moves into my chest, my heart beats rhythmically, calling out, reaching out its ever-expanding message of love and acceptance. My arms swing gently at my sides, joining the chorus of a body in motion.

Consciously, I open my senses to the surroundings. Breathing deeply, I smell a hint of moist earthy loam, followed by a whiff of pine, calming me even more deeply. The soft crunching of pine needles and oak leaves underfoot bring forth a chorus of shifting sounds to which the birds add their sweet notes. My eyes are soft, taking in the gray and brown textures of trunks, the tangle of huckleberry and wintergreen. Buds are swelling red on each branch tip. But most of all, my whole body is alive with energy, the energy extending from within, meeting the energy of the whole forest. This living being greets me, invites me, envelops me lovingly, so that little by little, I become part of this wholeness. My body boundaries dissolve. What is inner is also outer. What is outer is also inner. We are moving, living, dancing, walking, swaying, breathing as one huge loving being of light and beauty.

We move like this for a long time, endlessly communing: a rustle, a breath, a wind, a love, a warm and dappled light. Cautiously my balance gives way, shifting and changing, moving this way and that. I feel so full, so drunk with the beauty and radiant bliss of this moment. I feel like I could fly weightlessly. Gloriously, I am light filled. My awareness is less and less of form. I become so much less of an I and so much more of a wholeness. Love is everywhere, sustaining all of life in this moment. There is nothing but Totality, an immense experience of connectedness, an energetic primordial soup.

Gradually, after I don't know how long, differentiation returns. My body takes up space with weightedness. The trees, forest floor and tangle of life emerge. Songs return, the sunlight is warm and inviting. I stretch my arms upward to the clarity of blue sky, grateful for the vast immensity of space and mystery. I touch the Earth with the palms of my hands, fingers feeling the cool soft earth. I lean against a large oak, whose arms reach out in wonderment, carrying the weight of branches. I feel the texture of bark and the inner life of the tree streaming up and down. My energy roots into the dark folds of earth and rock. I am grateful for the solidity of support and base, grateful for the vast life bursting forth from Earth's glorious body. Reaching for the light, I open into the world of forest life with the assurance of innocence and newness. With care, I leave this forest, singing Her praises as I go, knowing that something has shifted deep inside my being. I thank Nature and all of these Forest Beings for welcoming me as part of this intricate web of life.

Into the Forest

Entering this forest with awareness,
breathing long deep belly breaths,
absorbing the scent of pine and moist earth,
hearing an occasional bird song,
experiencing the stillness of trees,
I bathe in the aliveness
of fresh bright green leaves.
Spring begins to dress herself,
celebrating the turn of Earth.

Opening my heart to the spirits of this place,
I feel their power,
sense their welcoming presence.
"I bring this small group trailing behind me.
Help us discover the sacredness of this place,
by moving us into a deep connection with you
within the Living Being of the Forest."

Tall dark green pitch pines
sway gently in soft wind,
filling us with a hint of warmth
while newly birth bronze oak leaves

flutter joyously.
Breath deepens in rhythm with walking slowly.
Balance improves as feet root into ground.
"To do" lists disappear
as busy mind settles into the present.
Shoulders drop.
Spine lengthens.
Gait relaxes into an easy glide,
feeling the flow of energy and light
moving through the body,
connecting Heaven and Earth.

Awareness opens the senses
to the excitement of discovery
engaging heart to heart.
Body boundaries loosen
as we settle into this moment
opening to the mysteries of forest life.

People say at the end,
"I will never experience the woods in the same way again."
"I am changed by this experience."
The Nature Spirits and Forest have worked their magic!

Creating a Song-line

Come walk with me
along the song-line of the heart
opening intimate relationships with trees, Earth, birds,
enchanting relationships
touching soul to soul.

The trail dips down from the muddy road
past the trail map,
past green briar.
Young oak and pitch pine
contribute needles and leaves underfoot
soft and scrunchy.
Stop a moment.
Breathe deeply
scenting pine filled cold damp winter air
feeling outward from the heart,
connecting into the energy of forest and dappled light.

The body bends a little forward,
breath quickens as we move up the rise
around the pine,
close to the large shapely granite stone
decorated with crusty gray green lichen.

Rounding the left going bend
the forest thickens,
a top-heavy pine has split from its base.
Nor'easter wind dance too much to bear.

The trail flattens
breath comes more easily.
I stop to raise my arms in gratitude,
to hear their whisper in return.
Listen carefully as they speak.
Wisdom echoes in their voices.
Heart-lines reach out
exploring connection.

The land becomes trough like,
once maybe an old road
traveled from bay and marsh
up the hill to Stony Brook.
The old stone wall tells tales
of horse drawn wagons bringing salt
to barrels and barrels of herring
up by the water wheeled mill
singing a corn grinding song.
Following the stones slightly downhill
to the masterful oak,
my dear friend sits in the middle of the roadway.
You can as I do,
stop to admire his beauty,
arms that extend out a short distance
then right angle upward
so strong

so beautiful.
Ask permission to touch,
slowly with heart feeling fingertips
sense bark grooved and pock marked
against smooth skin.
Acknowledging relationship,
he opens his heart
welcoming,
as we rest in mutual admiration.

The trail continues down along the wall
crosses it, then upward, cresting the hill.
Tips of marsh grasses below barely visible
as high tide full moon waters push upstream.
On the bank sits Grandmother Beech,
a dozen could hardly reach arms around
her myriad of trunks grown together
like one huge family.
In summer
her green canopy covers the sky, hides the marsh.
Throughout the valley so many beech babies have grown
bird planted.

Rest now,
breathe deeply,
feel into the sacredness of Earth, Forest and Marsh,
Sky and Human,
drink in Air and Light
sensing the Holiness of connection to all Life.

Early Morning Mists

The forest is blanketed
in early morning luminous gray.
Branch tips lay hidden
waiting for first light to find them.

Like a mystical Chinese brush painting
thick swirling mists
hint of great dark tree forms
emerging as if from another world.

Ocean waves barely seen,
wash against the sandy shore,
creating watery music
for the birthing of a new day.

What insights will emerge
out of these chaos filled days,
while we reach to embody
the presence of Being and the flow of Light?

Walking forward

touching ground consciously
feet sinking deeply into connection with Earth
breath enters the whole body
heart opens

light dances on the sandy forest floor
        creating dappled patterns
        in a community wind dance
tree leaves play restless music
        singing the forest into wholeness

walking among these tall beauties
                ears grow attentive to their stories
        feeling the strength of their presence
        reaching out with awareness
        embodying their invitation to connect
                some explore the intricacies and textures of bark
                        discovering many who make the tree their home
                some sense the internal complexity
                        feeling a movement not born of wind
                        a subtle liquidity of two bodies becoming one

this internal movement
like the swelling of waves
        the shifting of ocean currents
                shaped by contours of a sandy bottom
the pull of the moon
water being worked
                ethereally, mysteriously
residing deep inside the well of being

we stop
        gathering the forces of Earth in our palms
        pulling it up sideways
        reaching out into the green light of Nature
        bringing these energies up
        until fingers touch the sky
                and the golden light of the sun
        turning palms toward the crown
        our bodies are showered with this light, this energy
        we draw it deep into the marrow of our bones
                until we touch the Earth again.

embodying what we are experiencing
        walking with awareness,
extending our hearts, our love, the totality of who we are
        out into the being of the forest
connecting
dancing on a strand of the web of life
        supported and supporting
drunk from the intensity of
being an integral part of such a greater whole.

A young forest

The air is crisp and clear despite the warm rays of sun that cut through the bare gray bones of trees in early spring. This is young forest, for I heard it said that the man who once lived there could see the bay from his house overlooking cascading meadows down to the sea. The contours of the land were clear. The craggy places open to be seen. The twists and turns of the hillside revealed large boulders here and there dumped on these sandy shores thousands of years ago by a mile-high glacier. Chunks of ice dropped with such a force that ponds and lakes formed in the indentations, filling with glacial melt. The boulders carried here from far off places were dropped too, or perhaps gently placed as ice gave way to water in the warming times.

Young settlers saw forests filled with huge trees of many shapes and varieties. Industriously they cut them down for boats, houses, barns and winter heat. It is said that they burned 26 cords (1 cord=8'x4'x4') of wood a winter to stay warm in their drafty houses. A lot of trees fed that need, especially as settlements grew. At one point, there was nothing left but sand. The loam and rich forest floor were gone. Without foresight, they had used it all up. Farms were abandoned for lack of feed for cattle. Sand did not sustain a farm. When the winds blew hard, the sand piled up in the harbors. Fishing boats were compromised by shallower waters and overfished seas.

Cape Cod is on its third forest. A miracle of trees come to reclaim the land. The pitch pine is one of the first to take root, over time making a more harmonious and habitable bed for others to follow. Today, I look through this amazing young forest, mostly of oak and pitch pine and an occasional white pine or family of beech. How does it happen? All of these trees, the oaks in particular look to be maybe twenty or thirty years old. How did they all come to be here at around the same time? It certainly doesn't look like anyone went out and planted thousands of them. The occasional holly or special spruce or rhododendron definitely have the air of special placement, a loving hand who decided what and where to dig the hole to place a chosen one. These special ones have given birth to a few children who've grown up around the mother tree, still young and new and fresh, but not a thousand or more of oak.

I look out through this sea of gray tree bones with much gratitude for what looks like a miracle of birth: a huge forest, which now secrets the bay from view. I shift my focus to the boulder in front of me and gently place my hands on its crusty surface. Leaning over to look more closely, I see an amazing array of textures and shades of gray. At least three, if not four different kinds of lichen decorate its surface, while an occasional space opens up to reveal the subtle pinks, whites and grays of granite. Each of these patches of color and texture weave a beautiful tapestry covering the entire surface of this rock. I shift my attention to a deeper awareness of stone partially embedded in Earth. How much is hidden below the surface I do not know, but I feel into its solidity. Housed in Earth these rocks are the bones of the Earth helping to shape Her, providing contour and lifting Her skyward into ridges, hills and mountains. The energy here feels heavy but surprisingly airy. Touching the upper surface gives me commerce with the deeper hidden life, sensing ancient times of being carried aloft, dug out from some mountainside in Maine, now perhaps, still connecting with its origin. I rest here on its sloping side, lulled into a deep and dreamy place by the cool depths of its being, deeply resting.

Holy is Thy Name

There was absolutely nothing
    NO THING anywhere
    No sense of place
    No identification
    No Being
    No Time
Until the only way we can explain it
Some THING happened
An explosion so huge
Never known before
    Occurred.
Shards of Light flew everywhere
Sparks flew outward
LIGHT entered dramatically
    Creating space
    Creating direction
    Creating energy
    Creating contrast
Seeds of Light were scattered
Everything changed
Life began.

Now we don't think twice

Flowers kissed by bees and butterflies
Balance Male and Female power
Sun, rain, soil
Grow seeds until matured
Then taken up by wind, wing, fur
Or tossed by human hand
Planted
Nourished by Earth, Sky
In a Sacred Manner
Providing beauty and food.

A seed planted in the body of the Mother
Join male and female energies
Initiating life
Many kinds of life
Sustained and nourished.

A seed planted in the imagination
Nourished by internal creative juices
Fed by a sacred spring
Hidden deep within the Heart
Provides a mysterious opening
Into new possibilities
Bringing untold bounty into the world.

New shards of Light illuminate creation
Neither good nor bad
Birthing
Sustaining
Honoring Sacred Life
All born from a small seed.

Holy is Thy Name.

The Marsh and Wing Island

Tall green grasses wave back and forth on sunlit days,
short brushstrokes of grasses pushed this way and that by tidal waters
look like tousled hair, uncombed, unkempt.
So many shades and textures of green greet the eye,
moving from a tunnel of phragmites out
into a wide-open space of marsh
framed by creeks, sand dunes,
and the tree-lined shores of Wing Island.
Blue sky opens infinitely.
Heron and other water birds fish in the tidal streams.
Osprey, year after year, return to raise their young.
Small fish mature in protected spaces
while little crabs scurry in and out of grassy hiding places.
Crossing the marsh when tides are low,
weather worn wooden boards squish in receding waters
echoing sounds of footsteps.
This precious marsh home to many seen and unseen,
the pristine beauty of open space
makes me feel like I could fly free, up and out
circling round and round like a Red-Tailed Hawk,
heart free to roam untethered.

Moving from the vast open space of marsh
onto solid salt free land
embraced by the tunneled forest of Wing Island,
I turn right, away from the main thoroughfare
while others head to the beach
or learn about the particulars of woodland environments
or the mysteries of mudflats.
I choose the slow quiet magic of the secret path
safely guarded by two tall old cedars.
Pausing, breathing deep belly breaths,
I feel a sense of base, stability and connection into
Earth's strength of being
balancing the active nature of sky and sun,
both connect into the heart
energizing my whole being.
As I become aware of this living being,
this sacred forest reaches out to return the connection.
Together we are swimming in this vast sea
of trees, sand, creek, marsh and undergrowth.
Birds sing, while wind moves through trees,
sometimes softly
other times creating a loud cacophony of competing notes,
leaves rubbing, rattling, fluttering
mixing into a symphony of sound.
Sunlight and leaves create laced patterns
on the forest floor,
glittering, dancing, or utterly still.
I love this island that brings me such peace,
teaches me the profound lessons of connection
into the forest community,
a Mycorrhizal web embedded into the whole of life.

I come away knowing that I am not separate but an integral part
of the whole.
This beautiful Wing Island and marsh are a multifaceted classroom
where Nature teaches us unendingly, when we stop to pay
attention.

A choreographed poem

I stand in silence
slowly the wind raises my right arm
it flutters as if full of long white feathers
fingers flicker
then still again
my head turns slowly
gazing along the horizon of sea
gray today, mirroring storm driven clouds,
the left arm flies overhead quickly
turning the whole body
now focused on a ruffled horizon of green trees
dancing their own wind song
my hips shake back and forth
my trunk bending left then right
arms like wings pull me skyward
sailing on currents of wind.
Can I trust this new way of being?
This flight, untethered?

Letting go
I tilt my head back
arms extend out to each side

back arches
feet flow with grace
like ribbons on the long tail of a kite
out over the sandy beach I glide
below trails of seaweed pushed high by tide
decorated with seashells and glistening pebbles
create a necklace fit for the Goddess of the Sea
little lacy waves lick the shore
resist being pulled back out to sea again
I land softly at the water's edge
knees bending
body slowly curling
like a moon shell spiraling back in time,
I rock to the rhythm of wind and sea.

Beauty

a conversation that
opens the heart in awe
swallowing me whole
in the pure vast blueness of sky.
A spring flower gladdens my heart
providing a gateway
to the flowering of the Spirit.
Beauty opens awareness
to inner winds, skies and oceans
that speak a secret language to the heart.
Beauty, the golden key to the inner garden,
filled with unending abundance
flowing like a river,
pouring water over the edge of life,
cascading down into forever as Love.

Reaching below the surface

I touch your bark
my heart travels through my fingertips
entering your Sacred Being
awareness opens to Earth
recognizing the network of roots held there
lacing our energy together.
I welcome four new babies
weaving them into our growing family:
two pecans, two elderberries.
It feels like a birthday party.

I hear of so many wildfires burning
and it's just the beginning of June
skies turn orange
filled with the remnants of trees
now floating for hundreds of miles
settling onto the land and into our lungs.
What a sacrifice they make,
a red alert to a numb world of humans who
thoughtlessly toss cigarettes
igniting another fire so more trees die
raising Earth's temperature to a fevered pitch.

My bare feet converse with soil
and last year's pine needles
while walking along a woodland path
experiencing a depth of ground below the surface
as if reaching into Earth
acknowledging a joining within, not walking on.
Intimacy increases with each step, with each touch,
with leaning into a combined aliveness
recognizing connection
into this living community to which we belong.

Wisdom

Touch the intricate web of life
with heart love
just one strand vibrating
sets the whole world in motion.
Sing one note softly
from your heart
hear the Earth's symphony respond.
Wisdom comes
from ear to the ground
eye to the sky
heart opening awareness
to the flow of energy
greeting the moment.

The Hollow Bone

I am a hollow bone.
Your breath moves through me
        creating sound
        shrill notes
awakening those who can hear
awakening those who dance to Your music
        like the Sufi's turning and turning
        or the potter's wheel turning
until the turning brings us 'round right.
I move in this world quietly
        or not.
Your breath flows through my heart
weaving us together as One.
There are times when I throw up my hands in despair
Is there any hope?
A small whisper comes,
"You are born to this time of coming apart
you've been here before
there's no right or wrong
simply a coming apart
ride the wave
feel into the movement of wind

creating sound
creating Heart
creating an opening for those ready to open..."

Imagination

My heart catches fire
dropping embers into the belly
glowing.
Sparks of imagination spreading,
begin to sing.
What will come of it?
I close my eyes focusing inward.
Stars so bright against an inky inner sky
flow like a waterfall of infinite Light
through my being.
I open my wings
testing them against the wind.
Filling with air, each feather bears me aloft
beyond the boundaries of skin
beyond the boundaries of Earth
out past the silver of a half full moon.
Gliding fearlessly, softly, quietly
I see familiar bodies of land
surrounded by so much water,
huge sparkling blue oceans.
Rivers spread out in tangles
like elegant extravagant necklaces.

As I think about all of life that shares this home,
heart strings fly out
visibly attaching to this vast web of intricate life.
I cannot separate myself
even from the enthralling emotional roller coaster
spawned by those who love and those who hate.
My heart aches fiercely
then grows into quiet love,
extending, engulfing all that is.
Now is the time of coming apart,
chasms open up, giving view to inner depths
sometimes so dark my skin crawls,
tears stream down my cheeks.
I desperately want to look away
but I see threads of light and life everywhere
engaging curiosity and connection.
This Earth, this playground,
yearns for redemption
for unending love
transmuting horror into fodder for change
riding the waves of existence and grace.

Walking slowly,

very slowly.
Breathing moving in and out
Deeply.
Steps and breath become one rhythm.
Synchronistically arms, shoulders, hips sway
following an easy rhythm.
Feet caress the Earth.
Heart light expands beaming all the way around
joining the green light of Nature.
Energy of recognition sparks
connection with twin pine.
Flowing along the woodland path
like a cell in the blood stream of the forest,
hands extended become antenna.

Sensing the presence of the whole,
I slide into the living being of the forest
differentiation
no differentiation.
The fungal network webbed below
connects with my feet,
flowing within the soil,

flowing within my soul
connecting energetic currents of Being
filling with joy
delighting in this intimate dance
sunlight and shadow
warmth and coolness
soft and hardness
blend.
Love flows everywhere
as I enter the Heart of Creation....

A Forever Memory

Prayers intoned bounce off the polished blood red granite of the King's Chamber.
I lie down in the black basalt sarcophagus
entering the moment of Truth/Ma'at.
Part of me flies up through the shafts of starlight
high into the heavens above.
It is a holy moment of completion,
an ancient task left undone,
with no expectations.
After descending the steep wooden planks
under the corbeled ceiling of the Grand Gallery,
I crouch down
entering the narrow passage to the Queen's Chamber.
Intoned prayers continue.
The white limestone wall is rough to the touch.
Slowly slipping sideways,
my left leg lifts then spins me out into the small room.
My body begins to move without conscious thought.
Gradually awareness shifts, filling with Light
nothing but Light,
undulating like great waves of cosmic Northern Lights
an electromagnetic existence in energy

transforming everything....
no thoughts only experience
no physical form only Light.

I am totally transformed by this experience
no fear of death remains,
only a deep love and reverence for Holy Light.

Seeing Van Gogh's Stars

I whirl and twirl in tall grasses
under a blazing night sky,
whirl and twirl until tumbling
dizzy.
I fall on my back
looking at the sky,
squinting a little.
Stars giggle,
beginning to swirl into a thousand lights,
blues, reds, yellows and silver
dancing.
Lying still,
heart strings, like fishing line cast upward,
fling into the vast mysterious star sea
catching hold,
pulling me skyward to fly
along a stardust trail of phosphorescence.

Letting go, I float far and wide
inside Nut's star filled belly
until birthed with the sun.
I slide back home
in love with the wonders of Earth and Sky.
Meadow grasses tickle my heart.

Breathing

quietly into the heart
words form
fed by a silent stream of light
prayers speak then break apart
letters tumble down my body
feeding the Earth
waiting patiently in the stillness of winter
to plant new ideas supporting life
fresh sprouting visions of possibilities
to be nurtured in the sunlight of summer
gathering wisdom and strength
opening new spaces for exploring
while walking in the forest
or standing at the water's edge
listening to waves gently
wash against the sandy shore.

When mind and awareness mingle anything can happen.

I walk barefooted slowly down the forest path.
Breath fills my body as focus moves to the heart.
Every pore of my body opens out
into the Light of Awareness
singing in concert with forest life.
Aliveness is everywhere
with no difference between inside and outside.
I feel intricately woven
into an invisible flexible fabric.
My breath is tree breath.
My feet sink below the forest floor
webbing into the fungal network.
Nothing is personal
but a living, breathing, swaying, dancing
energy of interconnected aliveness.
Each part contributing to and vital to the whole
until there are no parts
just an energetic swirl and twirl of Totality.

The Heart, the Center of Life

I breathe deeply
        engaging Heart with inner awareness
        smiling opens the door
        compassion flows
        love without boundaries begins to spread
feeling expansion
        warmth
                sweetness
        moving from cell to cell
bringing forth joy, wonder, alertness,
openness to the adventure of life
        without prejudice.
Unbound
        energy flows beyond body boundaries.

Stopping by a tree I know
placing my hands gently on rough bark
fingers find purchase
the touch carries an invitation
        deep into the being of this oak
        one being connecting to another
        heart to heart
appreciation and gratitude flow

our roots lace up in mutual support
our arms and branches reach into vast blueness
        touching mystery
        touching fierce abandon,
                the fire of All of Life
connecting with so much heartfelt gratitude.

Looking into the eyes of my dog,
we see each other
        the energy of heartfelt love
        wraps around
        enveloping us
                in this quiet moment
        sharing appreciation
        trust
a bond
        looping gracefully around our hearts
paying homage to our deep loving connection

Extending fierce unbound love to a friend
        in a dark place
        suffering loss
                loss of hope
                loss of a dream
                loss of a miracle
                loss of a valentine unsent
        deep heart wrenching loss.
This love finds her frozen heart,
        reaching out I say without words,
"I am with you
I see and feel your pain
I offer unbound love."

Inspired by Rothko's Untitled Painting, 1952

I sit in the dark womb space of the kiva
extending awareness through the sipapu,
the small hole in the center of ground.
My umbilical cord connects to the placenta
resting bright orange in the belly of the Great Mother.
Bound are we in this birthing
as consciousness rises
emerging bloody orange
into another life
gifted with deep awareness born of Earth.

As consciousness rises
form releases into textured lavender fields
of energy and light with breath.... vibrating
moving as electromagnetic currents
like great tidal waves of luminous northern lights.
Love flows endlessly
as consciousness rises
knowing no bounds
becoming the totality of One Living Being.

The song of the Wood Thrush

sings my heart wide open
lifting my body into the lightness of Being
to sail on a luminous sea of delight
connecting into a world filled
with the aliveness of green,
and earthy smells.
Beauty is everywhere.

Sunlight slips through leaves

streaming tendrils of yellow
reaching to bathe the Earth in first Light.
I imagine myself standing waist deep in pond water.
Warm and inviting
my feet squish into the muddy bottom
planting themselves.
An energetic tap root extends downward
making its way through layers of fertile ground
deepening connection, centering me into Earth's Heart.
Roots begin to spread outward
creating stability.
Root toes join with the mycorrhizal network.
This base, this network,
this love resonating from Earth's Heart
flows upward through squishy mud,
rising into the green stem of legs into the body.
Arms reach out on either side.
Hands morph into great round green leaves.
Like solar panels, they absorb the power of the sun,
feeding the heart, feeding the body
birthing a huge flower above my head.
One funnel shaped petal opens at a time

until a fully formed white lotus blossom
rests at my crown.
Heavenly light flows down through petals
into the green seeded trumpet in the center
surrounded by a magnificent golden fringe.
Heavenly Light soaks into my body,
rooting it into ground
while transporting moisture upward
releasing particles of Holy Love into a hungry world.

Walking

down the woodland path,
I gather the green of trees,
soak in the songs of birds,
cloak myself in the flutter of leaves and wind.
Mosaic patterns of leaf and light
decorate the forest floor.
A large granite rock returns a smile
as I pass slowly by.
Stopping by an old friend
in the middle of the path,
I take off my shoes
to stand next to him
feet sinking into soft cool spongy moss.
Offering the palms of my hands,
I graciously touch his bark
feeling into his solidity and strength.
The soles of my feet extend downward
through the layers of humus, sand and rock
like a huge tap root running parallel
to the underground growth of tree root.
There's a depth of ground and connection
a solidity comes into my being, resting.

Awareness recognizes energy being drawn upward,
as I feel into the blue sky and
touch the warmth of sunlight.
As the tree and I stand parallel to one another,
the hardness between us begins to soften
until there's a continuous experience
of joining with no separation
but a watery wave like pulse
moving vertically through us.
Unknown words form,
tumble out of my mouth
like a shared sacred prayer,
then all is still again.

My heart

made of star dust
spirals around like the Milky Way
moving in on itself
creating space
creating center
giving room for the flow of swirling blood,
generating immense magnetism,
the profound energy of compassion,
a vast connection
    to life
    to mystery
    to deep love.
Like mycelium with threads of light and energy,
my heart reaches out
    informing
    being in-formed
    by all of life.

When I was in my mother's womb,
I swallowed the Milky Way
    becoming Light
    entering the spiraling Heart center of Being.

A spiral dance

Tree bodies
Our bodies
build on spirals
Like the shapes of conch shells
mirroring Fibonacci sequences.
How do I experience the flow
of light
of blood?
Breathing into electromagnetic currents
the body disappears.
I become undulations of Light
no body just light
nothing static
shaping me constantly.

I don't want to walk in a straight line
but weave like a brook
winding its way through the forest
its path shaped
by land
by rock and soil
by trees, roots and cliff.

Eddies of water catch leaves
twirling them around
tumbling
talking
moving
gurgling
foaming
circulating up down around
water ways spiraling
gathering strength
carrying stories from up in the mountains
of springs
of deep wells of water
fed by winter snows and ice
enlivened by passage through shapes of landscape.

Life is like that
Tributaries of experience
feed the growing story of life lived
and experienced.
Nothing in isolation
shaped by trees,
animals,
people,
circumstances

Boulders that impede
where we thought we were going
                    head us off in another direction
stories spun from encounters
surprising twists and turns
            a joining
               a releasing
                  a gathering
                    a touching
influences shape our dance of life
            shift it
               change it
as the internal spiraling of the heart
      fills us with love
and love released out into the world
            touches and being touched by constant movement
even in the quietest moments
            the heart,
               the breath
dancing through our bodies
            minds
                        spirits
connecting us always to the spiraling flow of the Milky Way
            and beyond
                           and into
life as a sacred mystery
            constantly being informed by lived experiences.

In the neighborhood

I slip out of the house
while most of the world is still asleep.
Gray light pervades
black tree bodies
intricate outlines inked
against first light
stand sentinel
within this small community.
Their living presence
completes a wholeness.
Houses are tucked among trees,
gardens, lawns
but it's the tall bare trees
that define the space
give it character and regal beauty
even when leafless.

To sit with illusion

and not get swallowed up by it,
so compelling, pushed by the dance of planets.
Pulling up the curtain on the day's drama
to see through the reeling world,
beyond the push and pull
well-orchestrated by those invested
in creating seductive chaos.
The sun rises every day.
Light pours out, bathing this Earth
saturating plants and trees
encouraging bird songs and peepers
filling our hearts with luminous possibilities.
Our heart light shines forth
singing joyously, dancing,
ferociously writing,
fired up with ideas,
or sitting quietly under a favorite tree
or on a sandy beach
listening to the eternal lapping
of waves against the shore.
Tides move in and out
seasons change

the moon grows full then disappears again.
Life moves on in spite of all the drama.
We can choose how we live it.

Coloring up

Driving up the west coast
we discovered a jewel
tucked into the top of an old volcano
a lake so deep its bottom unknown
its color turquoise
as deep a greenish blue as the best of stones.
Making my way down the steep path
I dove into the cool water
and turned entirely turquoise.

Today walking in the woods
bathing in the lush late spring woodlands
I turn completely green
fed inside and out by the forest.

Standing close to a tree
leaning into her deeply rooted strength,
I become powerful oak presence.
With open hearts
we swim together in green sweetness.
Orion, my dog, sits close
watching carefully

opening his heart into that communion
inspiring stillness.
Peace arises.

As the day draws softly to close
I dream sweet turquoise/green dreams
while swimming in Divine lush Oneness.

Full Moon to Earth

I dress myself in translucent radiant Light,
a gift from dancing with the Sun.
I look down on beautiful blue Earth
as one goddess to another.

She radiates deep pains of labor,
gut wrenching difficult labor.
What will be born of it?
The elements gather around Her
Fire, Air, Water, Earth.
Her belly begins to roll.
She burns with feverish struggle,
twisting and turning.
Her water breaks flooding the land.
What will be born of it?

I send moonbeams of heart light
to soften the pain.
I tell her how much I appreciate
Her courage
Her depth of vision.
I bathe Her in gossamer Light
whispering lullabies
soothing Her struggles,
sending Her the energy of Love.
What will be born of such a labor?

The Inconceivable

Deep in the forest
my heart opens wide,
extends far beyond body boundaries,
touching trees,
every plant, every bush, every flower.
The song of the Wood Thrush
spins my soul lifting with love
so high into the heavens
it's inconceivable.
The rich loamy scent of forest earth
soft to the touch under my feet
invites connection in and out
along the fungal threads.
Perhaps like the Navaho woman
who having invented weaving,
became so intrigued with her craft,
they found her woven into her creation.
I, too, am woven into the threads of forest life
into the vast mycorrhizal and rooted networks of earthly life,
into the puffy white clouds and blue sky,
into the golden rays of sunlight,
the soft embrace of the moon,

the intricate web of stars sparkling.
The undulating energy of love
welcomes me into all of life.

Seeking treasures

I walk into the lost and found
looking for treasures.
Encountering this unknown sea
            a smile spreads
            the breath deepens
            bellows of the belly fire up the heart,
awareness awakens discovery.
I open a new book,
a treasury of words
describing landmarks.
It's not about dancing, but I think of it that way
            experiencing body,
            breath,
            space
pointing to relationships.
I imagine dancing on a strand of webbing,
a tightrope
connected.
I move and am being moved
            by trees
            by wind
            by waves of salty icy sea

by the eyes of my dog, his soft fur
by deep drifts of snow
by the wonder of friendships.
Which way to turn, which way to twist?
I smile
opening heart to the flow of life
dancing on the web of interconnectedness
one step
one turn
one twirl follows the next
influenced by,
in relationship with life's treasures
an improvisation
creating infinite presence.

A Spiral of Stones

In the woods behind the house
at the center of a circular carpet of moss
white pebbles worn smooth by an ancient sea
move in spirals outward
from a cluster of clear quartz crystals.
I come to sit here in early morning light.
Fingers of yellow and white sunlight
reach for the forest floor
tumbling down over branches of beech and sycamore.
Old Tom turkey gobbles up on the ridge
while Wood Thrush sings fluted notes from Heaven
and Pileated Woodpecker taps away loudly nearby.

Embraced by green
I shift my focus to an inner awareness.
My breath takes on an even flow,
deepening.
Shoulders relax.
Body opens up
making room for a larger heart space.

Extending my awareness into the Earth,
She feels soft and inviting.
Our combined energies flow slowly up my spine.
What was solid becomes a continuous liquid wave.
My head shakes rapidly back and forth.

Silence seeps into my bones,
my jaw goes slack
opening the mouth,
the breath stops,
my body fills with light
gradually shifting to starlit spacious darkness.

I lose all sense of inner and outer.

I am in the Awareness of Totality.

Heart light, no light

Space, no space

Time, no time

So very sweet.......

Presence

so elusive
touches me deeply for a moment
        then I run away
an extraneous thought
somehow more compelling
until once again I find my breath
        focus awareness
        root into ground
        open quietly.
Such magnificence
comes and goes so easily,
like a skilled intimate dance partner
touching in for a moment of grace
        until I stumble
        or look away distracted.

I crave the soft easy glide
the intimate connection
        two as one
        breathing as one
moving across the dance floor
of the Universe without differentiation
sustained with skill.

In the beginning

as I enter the fire of becoming,
my heart grows large
filling with primordial Light.
It is the First Day
when all is raw, new, fresh, unencumbered.
I break out of the egg
with the courage of being present;
space opens;
the deafening roar of heart and blood softens.
I settle into the stillness of new.

Ground provides a center point,
holding me, calming me.
I stretch out my arms,
hands feel the weight of air,
the warmth of sunlight,
the cool texture of Earth.
I feel the thrum of Her heartbeat
vibrating through my body
waking up an aliveness.

An invisible web of connection
sings strands vibrating,
creating immeasurable comfort and grace.
Being held, without being held.
Being supported and supporting,
touching and being touched.
Textures of life are everywhere
weaving me into ancient wisdom.

The Delicious Present Moment *

has been powered up by rich dark brown coffee.
I sit with focus
diving into this moment
        better than walnuts and steel cut oats
        better than beating myself up
        for ego spilling over into conversations.
Drinking in the coolness of air,
connecting into the Field with friends,
opening to a heart full of tears,
expanding awareness
opening beyond the expected
        into the unknown bliss of this moment.
Stepping off my high horse
        coming to ground
the inner/outer fire flows stronger.
Primordial energy flows,
letting go of yesterday's garbage
slowly sinking into the sweet smelling
        deliciousness of this moment.

* Inspired by Cathy Kreyche

The sun rises in my spirit,
my body shakes,
the tongue whispers a secret language,
boundaries disappear.

For the Friends of Wing Island

I hover over the marsh and Wing Island
admiring a green mantle
of intricately woven wild marsh grasses
tall, short, thick and rich.
Some grasses follow the tidal streams.
Others spread out across the wetland
creating ruffled textures and tasseled fringes.
These provide protected birthing places
for crabs, snails and fishes,
feeding places for heron and water birds,
protection for town and wildlife
from wanton storm surges and rising king tides.

When tides are low
a simple walkway gives passage to Wing Island.
Groundsel and high bush blueberries
create a magical tunneled entrance
into a sweet forest of pine, oak, sassafras and cedar.
Secret trails illuminate the interconnectedness of all of life
while others go straight to the beach
to the mystery of mud flats and beauty of Cape Cod Bay.
Nature's treasured classroom has so much to teach.

With the Devas and Nature Spirits
I gather Light
threads of gold, green, blue and silver
to weave an invisible cloak of protection,
like a huge ocean-going fisherman's net
tossed over island, beach and marsh.
Edges are anchored along the perimeter
into the mycorrhizal network of underground life.

If you close your eyes
you can see it floating, hovering with sparkling magnificence
filling spaces with even more Light
protecting, energizing,
letting the wild things be wild,
letting children and adults be schooled in partnership with Nature
experiencing their dance on the Web of Life.

Now I weave those threads of light into our group
reminding us why we've joined together
and the importance of the work that awaits us.
Grounded in marsh and woodland
we're as fragile and complex an ecosystem
as the one we've gathered to protect.
Our hearts, each manifesting their own skill,
are compassed toward a common cause.
Let our light shine brightly
weaving us back together
to rally to the beauty and innocence
of that for which we work to protect.

I am

spanda, softly pulsing through my body
fed by breath
promoted by root
aligned with heart, aligned with crown.
This plumb line frees the movement of energy,
the flow of Light.
Space opens up full circle
no body boundaries
breath stops.
Light radiates down from the crown,
serpentine energy caresses my body.

I am a connector
weaving works of magic
connecting Heaven and Earth
with flowing Light.

I am a connector
opening hearts to the Heart of the Earth,
weaving people into the forest
into the fullness of the Living Being of Nature.

I am threads of fungus,
mycelium wrapping around root toes
connecting sustenance, intelligence, information
into the community of Wholeness.

With gratitude and deep abiding Love,
well rooted, I am called to Heavenly Light.
I bring a sweet energy, words of magic
flooding the world with Light
helping to weave Divine Presence
into the fabric of All that Is.

Illusion

Caught in a huge tidal wave
gasping for air
rolling around
ground into sand
looking up through the green glass of sea
desperately seeking the light of the Sun,
body pushing hard, legs kicking, arms flailing, lungs burning.
Then there is no breath, no sense of time.

Sometimes, when I lie awake at night
old memories unbidden flood my mind,
tears spilling as I scroll through the litany of regrets.
I want to let go of the need
to push, to strive, to be right, to be forgiven.

Yesterday walking the woodland trail on Wing Island
where the Nor'easter blew hard,
toppled trees lie still, gradually rotting,
giving their lives back to the soil,
enriching underground forest life, their babies and Earth.
Even in death there is a peaceful purpose,
no striving, no pushing, no resisting, just Being.

I begin to see this trail of regrets
as just another phase of letting go of the illusion
of being right or wrong, good or bad.
Perhaps I can move to just being present, finding love
in the undulating evening song of crickets and peepers,
in the glory of the setting sun as it kisses the trees good night,
in the sweet patience of my dog
as we take our good night stroll around the block.
He stops and listens. He stops and listens.
I need to listen to the settling of evening moving into night.

The Queen of Night

enters, dramatically emerging
from behind the curtain of Earth,
slowly slipping upward
gradually revealing her full form.
The brightest stars Her only companions.
Her smiling presence glowing.
Her soft golden white garments flow outward
embracing Earth
illuminating night.
Peepers and crickets loudly sing Her praises
as trees dance gracefully to soft wind music.
Bears, bobcats and deer seek food by Her night light.
Immense power hides
behind Her sweet smile and beneficent eyes.
Tidal waters respond to Her tug
pushing waters high up on the shore
creating necklaces of shells, seaweed and brightly colored pebbles
to mark the water's reach.
Human emotions run at a high pitch.
Women are pulled into monthly cycles.
More babies are born.
Energy abounds.

In gratitude for the beauty and power of the Queen of Night
let's dance to honor Her magical Light
as it swirls and twirls,
embracing us in Heavenly delight.

Winter Solstice

the still point
manifesting the beauty of starlit nights
        of snowflake mystery
        of restless trees
as the North wind pushes through leafless branches.
The sun slowly drops over the horizon
taking a last bow
it touches the tops of trees
lighting up bare branches in warm peach and
flashing rosy red onto the underbellies of gray clouds.
The cold night sets in.

We've come to walk the labyrinth.
Embracing the circle, lights twinkle,
as one by one we enter the serpentine path.
Ritually, my breath sets an internal rhythm.
My body knows this ancient route
honoring the turning of Earth
honoring the cycles of Sun
honoring great star-studded Orion
climbing out of the celestial sea
to be birthed again and again and again.

Faithfully followed by bright star Sirius
showing us the way home.
The ancestors are with us
opening the gate of becoming.
What mystery will emerge
from the darkness of this night?

Winter trail

The trail winds through an oak forest.
Dank smells of moist earth,
an occasional whiff of pine,
startlingly red and yellow acorns dot the trail.
A tangle of green briar
offers a leafless thorny curtain.
Three mottled red orange leaves
hang on a low-lying huckleberry,
a reminder of season's passing.

Leaves now released
reveal the intimacy of the forest.
Earth's inner shape caught in
a rise of land marked by
huge granite stones
dropped here thousands of years ago.
An occasional white pine, fir and holly,
or emerald mosses brightening the folds of land.
This forest has taken off her outer clothing
showing off the detailed beauty of her skin.
I'm tempted to push past the stone wall
to wander off the path into the glen

or over the rise of hill
or simply to find a sweet spot
to sit and feel
the cool moistness of Her body
sharing heart
sharing presence
sharing an intimate connection.

Gray upright tree bones

connect earth and sky.
Huge stones anchor stillness.
Green pines whisper silently.
A sleepy forest giant
beckons,
"Sit with me.
Listen to my breath.
Know that I'm alive in you,
singing the light of creation
of beauty
of joy
of passion
of life fully lived
of heart flowing open
streaming sweet melodies of Truth
endlessly."

In an Old Story

Clouds hover overhead
like mysterious mountains in an ancient landscape
now set against a baby blue sky.
Golden rays of light
flood the landscape
lighting tree trunks lemon yellow
inviting light to flow
through plants, humans, all life.
Woven are we with flowing light,
the weft threads,
into the Wholeness of Being.

In an old story
sky was separating from Earth
slowly
gradually
imperceptibly at first.
But the animals noticed
and were alarmed.
What to do?
Each took a turn, volunteering,
trying to attach it again

and each failed.
They laughed at spider,
the smallest of all,
who said, "I can do it."
When there were no other choices
she created a thread
tossing it from Earth to Sky
attaching
climbing.
From Sky to Earth
another thread
back and forth back and forth.
"You pull from that side,
we'll pull from this side."
Animals lined up, pulling
straining
cooperating.
Gradually threads tightened
weaving Sky back to Earth.

Shades of Gray

shimmer the pond
        water reflecting
a scrim of light gray sky onto which is cast
    occasional raggedy dark clouds
sliding hurriedly by
    scattering translucent rain drops
        falling through
    great gray black tree sculptures
        leafless,
    lichen ladened
    standing quietly in early morning light,
woven into a winter fabric
    of subtle beauty and peacefulness.

Hovering
    just under the horizon
        Sun flushes the sky pink
opening fissures of turquoise
    as pink fades into light creamsicle orange.
As the sun crests Earth's boundaries
    tree crowns turn gold
        gradually filling their bodies with color
    streaking gray trunks with lemon yellow.
Damp wetland Clethra turns deep red
    as the world wakes up
        coloring a new day full of promise.

A gift arrives

an exchange they say
for love and support
from the heart
given freely in hard times.

Beautiful books of Lost Words,
a precious reminder of those Beings
now lost to the English dictionary
sacrificed
for techno speak.
What happens when words of wonder
words illuminating species are lost
to the imagination
to the World of Named Things
exiting definition and experience
into nonexistence?
When they describe a way
of being
of living
of beauty
erased from the Web of Wholeness.
Are we emptying the Natural World,
replacing it,
vivifying technology,

in a stark cold description
as a way of being?
As species disappear from Earth's vocabulary
how will future generations be enriched
without red fox, barn owl, moth,
adder, or acorn
to name but a very few?

Dusty and worn
tattered tomes
unearthed a thousand years from now
in a remote archeological dig
are discovered.
Wonder arises,
who are these beautiful creatures
who once roamed the World
and the English language?
Lost words found again
honored
with beauty and celebration
with immense gratitude for elegant retrieval.

Winter Magic

Looking out my window
snowflakes flutter and dance
        gracefully,
        landing their crystals selves
        one on top of another.
Out of the back of the wardrobe I go...
        soft silky fur coats,
        smelling slightly of expensive perfume,
        brush my cheeks
        as I push past to unlock the door.
Moving into a white world
        tumbling with snowflakes
        I swish, twirl and swirl
                fall down
                roll
                get up
                        round and round 'til dizzy
                        cheeks flush red.
Then sitting in stillness
        I watch this winter wonderland,
        smelling the cool earthiness of winter pine.
        Catch snowflakes on my tongue
        melting their intricate designs,

        tasting the cold wetness.
Trees fill up with whiteness
        blown against their trunks
        smooth white against rough dark bark
        drawing a line on top of fallen trunks
        creating a painting of white on black.
Puffs of white decorate each delicate burst of pine needles
        only to be fussed away
        as wind dances these soft, regal beauties.
Walking again
        snow crunches underfoot
                stepping
                sinking
                lifting.
Movement of rabbit, coyote, deer, bird becomes visible.
        Deer dance in a circle,
                prancing
                playing.
        Rabbits run with wide leaps
                from one hiding place to the next.
I follow the coyote trail.
        They stop and sniff
        join friends enthusiastically.
Forest life made visible.

Fingers begin to numb,
Nose reddens,
Snow down my boots,
fur coats call
back I go.
How nice to choose
when to open that magic door!

Heart's Light sings a Love Song

loud and clear
confetti flung out into the universe
a celebration of human possibilities.

This world darkens
  to much stress and strain
  to much anger
  to many lies
  to much need for power and wealth.

Nothing to do but rest
  in the magnificent fountain of everlasting love
    for the magic of snowflakes creating a white world
    for the beauty of loving connections of with family
    and friends
    for the magnificent love shared along the delicate
    strands of life connecting life
  to revel in joy,
  to dance to the tune of the expanding heart
  to sing, write, paint of what we know,
  bathing in the Light of the never-ending river of graciousness
    full of radiance
adding this piece to the pie of creation
  balancing what is.

Tree

voices restless
thick with words
under full moon's light
mark snow filled days danced and gone.
Sun melts the glory of white
for a day or two
as temperatures rise
then fall
rise then fall.
Perhaps trees share their annoyance
over brusqueness of change, saying
"Take me by the branch tip
swing me round and round
bend my trunk this way and that,
just because you can.
Roots laced up,
we'll share the load.
We'll sing your music,
dance to the raucous tune
of bend and bow
twist and turn.
We'll remain elegantly strong
enjoying the ride
as white winter moves slowly
into budding bright green spring."

Dancing in the Streets: *histories of collective Joy**

sets my feet tapping.
As ice slicked Susan Lane
circling our sweet neighborhood begins to melt,
people gather.
So many have been invited:
        Hafiz, Rumi, the Sufis
        Fancy dancers
        Hopi Rattlesnake dancers
        Celtic Beltane maypole dancers
        Rabbits, Deer, Coyotes, Turkeys.
Wild Things join the circle.
The whole neighborhood
readies for celebration and fun.
Trees whisper a wind song,
birds join in,
crickets and peepers punctuate the rhythm
        feet are tapping
        wings are flapping
        earthworms wiggle from side to side.
This celebration of community
        of life

* Ehrenreich, Barbara. *Dancing in the Streets: histories of collective joy*, A Holt paperback, 2006.

of wholeness
fills the hearts
creating song
creating an orchestra and chorus
        of music and dance
a magnificent rhythm emerges.
People,
all kinds of people
join hands, wings, paws, fins
singing, dancing
round and round the circle they go.
A cloud of Joy arises
filling the air
spreading out over the bay, the ocean
        whales dance
        cod dance
        sharks and lobsters dance
        kelp sways back and forth.
The world shakes and shimmies in deep heartfelt Joy.
A celebration
        of the marvelous intricacies of creation,
        even the sun and stars shine and twinkle
in the infinite expression of Divine Oneness.

Not quite time

The new moon heralds a new cycle.
I long to work fingers into soil
even though very cold days are on their way.
Sorted seeds could be started inside
but it's not time yet.
Days are quiet
not yet filled with the busyness of Spring.
I sit by the fire knitting,
peacefully finishing what I started long ago,
before there's no time.

Earth hovers in this in between place
soil not warm enough.
Roots reaching out seek sustenance,
seek water, warmth and connection,
but are suspended.
Some daring green shoots begin to show.
Snow drops hang unopened.
Cold days hover around the edge
waiting for a seat at the table
waiting for one more frigid blast
waiting for permission to let go
to give into warmth and ease.
It's just not time yet.

Spring is playing

hard to get.
She's begun to put on a few fancy clothes
fringed with yellow daffodil ruffles.
She flirts with sun filled bright blue days
but Winter says, "Oh no such luck!"
and tugs her back with chilly winds,
clouds and more rain.
"No thoughts of celebration for you yet."
Peepers pretend she's already here
drowning out her fickleness
with loud courting songs that fill the air.
The birds completely ignore
her wavering commitment
too busy flirting,
singing sweet notes of enticement
while charting out their territories.

I just want to be warm.
The wood stove fire burns brightly,
heavy blankets piled one on top of the other
weigh me down into deep dreams.
Layers of sweaters and warm jackets
remind me to go slow

enjoy the still quiet days
not yet filled with outside chores.
There's time to read,
write some poems,
paint a watercolor or two.
I need to bundle up,
take some nice long slow woods walks,
breath in the fresh cool air,
enjoy early spring surprises
like pretty little purple Heal-All flowers
peeking out from clumps of grasses still asleep.
Nature certainly doesn't need me to push Her along.
Spring honors the pace she needs
to manifest with love all of the beauty that will follow.

Spring is Coming

bird feeders empty quickly
finches begin to blush yellow
crocuses push through late snow
spring whispers in the air.

Woodland air is sweet
bright moonlight creates dark lines
of tree shadows across the path
the raspy fox bark eerily fills the night.

Sitting at the Temple of Light
sparkling crystalline energy swirling,
stars twinkle through dancing branches.
Trees wink a secret language
known to only a few.

I hunker down
watching, listening, feeling
the mystery unfolding in my heart
birthing seeds of possibilities
to be planted in the spring.

A thick spring snow

tumbles down from the heavens
as if someone up there's spring cleaning
        shaking out all of the feather pillows
        covering Earth,
        momentarily dressing her up in white.
Anxiously waiting for warming sun,
        bright days
        buds to show off
        their little yellow faces,
I sort my seeds
        what gets planted as soon as the hoe can dig,
        what starts in indoor flats,
        what waits for spring, summer or fall.
How sweet to touch the seed sowing soil
        pressing the earth
        laying seeds down one by one.
Firewood stacked on the porch
        is almost gone
        making room for a greenhouse.
Hydrangeas and fruit trees have been given their hair cuts.
Dry stems and empty seed heads
        from last years flower beds

trimmed back.
I'm ready to call in the Nature Spirits
to begin our garden work
Ah, but not quite yet,
patience for the slow handing off of winter's wand
to be passed on to spring's eagerness
to green up the world.
How blessed are we to have garden beds
and chickens laying colored eggs
when so many suffer so
scrounging for food
searching for water fit to drink
watching their homes and land destroyed.
There's so much heartache in this world
put there by someone else's greed,
so much inequality, hurt and pain.
Can we humans ever create peace on Earth?
Maybe world peace begins at home
in our hearts
in everyone's heart.
A fantasy far from current reach.
Breathe and smile
shining forth the inner heart light
sending Love throughout the world.

March Madness

March maidens dance with glee,
a teasing testimony of fickleness,
to sweet songs of birds
full throated in their belief that spring is coming.
"Spring is coming!!" they sing convincingly
amid snowflakes and fierce cold winds.
The last Hoorah, for Earth knows Her rhythmic pulse.
In Her dark and thawing soil
seeds begin to wiggle,
roots drink deep draughts of nourishing rain.
The Sun shines brighter
sending warm rays of Hope.
People sort their seeds,
plan their gardens,
dream of burgeoning beds of bright beauty
and rows of delicious vital vegetables.
As March, inevitably moves on
the New Moon shows her promising smile.
Seeds get planted in flats, snuggled in greenhouses,
dreaming of yet bright blue skies warm summer breezes
and songs of buzzing relatives paying homage to their beauty.
So march on you maidens of change,
we know your hearts are full of gladness
for the promises that you bring.

Let in the Light

open the door
pull back the curtains
the sun is shining!

Watch wind gently pushing pond water
deliciously shimmering sunlight
sending thousands of sparkles
out into the world.

Build a fire in the wood stove,
draw a chair up close,
soak in the warmth,
gaze deeply into dancing light.

Smile a big smile.
Feel the door of the heart
open wide, beaming
light from the inside out.

Revel in the sweet beauty of Light.

At Spring Equinox

rays of sunlight quicken Earth as
Holy Light flows into Her Body.
Earthworms wake up
wiggle to the surface
to bask in golden light.
Daffodil buds swell
preparing to sound their trumpets
declaring Light and Life flows through all things.
Like Hafiz, I want to cover you with Light
to experience rays of Holy Light
descending from crown rooting into Earth
so we can dance in Harmony and Truth.

The sun is shining
the light is golden white
soaking into soil
inspiring birth
flowing into broad tree limbs
encouraging the swelling of buds
fingers itch to turn over fertile soil
create row after row
planting seeds

making a garden of overflowing bounty.
I watch artichoke babies
having sprouted their first true leaves
stretch toward the light.

We dance a chaotic Earth dance
singing loudly of what we see and feel
holding in our hearts the possibilities
of new found paths, moving in concert
with Holy Light into times of Peace and Beauty
that seem so far away.

The reluctance of spring

I want to leap joyously
into the warmth of spring
but feel caught mid-air
spun round six times
landing in a sun filled day,
but the cold wind catches me up short
seeping into my bones.
Birds sing voluptuously
partnering up
building nests.
The new moon has arrived.
I want to dig compost into the soil
plant peas
transplant blueberries and flowers,
a cold wind pushes my foot
down hard on the brake.

After so many cloud filled nights
the sky now cold and clear
wondrously filled with stars,
the sky map writes me home
deep into the heart of longing.

Settling in as warmth spreads
from the wood stove fire
bright glowing embers crumble and shimmer
lighting up my heart, softening my gaze.
Smiling in gratitude for the cheer
for the warmth
for the gift of glowing sparks
that will feed my dreams,
I'll save my spring dance for another day.

In the afternoon several days later,
despite the chilly wind,
the sun's warmth finds me in the garden
raking compost into raised beds
preparing for planting.
Finally, fingers touch cool earth
sweeping the soil back and forth
carving indented rows
first placing carrot seeds
then lettuce
then fava beans
then snow peas
carefully covering them.
Patting down the soil
I sing softly good cheer and growing songs
nestling those babies into the womb of Mother Earth.

Inside, filling small pots
tomato,
cucumbers,
leeks,

and eggplant
pressing tiny seeds one at a time into seed starting soil
sprinkling them with water
carrying them to a sunny spot
I wait patiently for signs of green sprouts.
The Spring ritual of planting has begun.

The night air, finally still,
is soft, fresh and clean.
Spring peepers fill the air
with whispered textures of song.
The hazy white horns of moon
embrace the silhouette of the whole
accompanied by bright Goddess Venus
dancing directly below.

What a celebration of life's beginning,
inviting the swelling of buds
and the surfacing of dandelion greens
opening the doorway to beauty
happy for the ritual of Spring
and the beginning of another cycle.

Spring

finally decided to move in her furniture.
Splashes of bright orange and yellow,
a loud distinctive call,
announces Orioles have arrived
seeking oranges and grape jelly.
The timid hummingbird flashing iridescence
sips and runs
seeking the next sweet, tasty spot.
Maples hang their bright red fringes,
seeds that will seek a twirly planting.
Bright sunshine,
warm air,
a good spring rain
washes us clean
feeding the little plant babies
turning the world green.
Trees leaf up,
except of course the oak,
last to join the party and last to leave.
Please place the furniture carefully,
we want you to stay.
To long you've flirted

move in,
not move in,
the cold north wind reluctant
to give you enough space
to put down your roots.
We celebrate your gifts of warmth, rain and light.
How happy we are to plant our seeds in warm soil
and move greenhouse babies out into the garden.

Fresh Leaves

birthed in warm sunlight
push out from the ends of each tiny twig.
Red maple blossoms now cover the ground
making a speckled carpet.
As daffodils begin to fade,
tulips readily take their turn
in the fancy Spring parade.
Chartreuse willow branches
filled with tiny new leaves,
drape gracefully into the landscape.
The rich scent of pine and fresh sun fills the air.
Evergreens thick and supple, dance constantly,
choreographed by wind: up, down, in and out,
creating a mixing bowl of movement.
Huge andromeda in full bloom
offer waterfalls of cascading blossoms,
looking like a mysterious landscape painting.
To all of the fresh new colors and wind inspired dances,
the birds add a spirited symphony of call and response,
enthusiastically announcing their presence.
Happily the natural world is waking up.
I drink in the movement with my body,

drunk with the ecstasy of this moment.
Heart strings connect, move, integrate
into the force of new life all around.
So in love am I with the fabric of woodland life
tears well up,
words silently form in my mouth
overflowing with immense gratitude
honoring Earth, Sky, Sun, and the glory of Spring.

There's a party going on!

Trees dress up in bright new gowns of green.
Flashes of yellow, red, orange and black
flit busily back and forth from Nature's Wild Garden.
Swamp maples dress in dangling fringes of deep red,
while oaks show a more subtle bronze.
Cherry lays a tapestry of puffy clouds of pink blossoms
against a vast expanse of a cobalt blue sky.
Bouquets of flowers decorate every nook and cranny
with yellows, whites, purples, reds.
Young and middle-aged White Pine
dance ceremoniously in long silky green skirts,
while tall elders gently sway this way and that
to the soft melodious tune of the wind band,
breathing through harps of needle and branch,
harmoniously humming the forest alive.
Enthusiastically birds add their songs,
creating a lively spring symphony.
Cloud angels join the parade across the sky
dressed as prehistoric feathered dinosaurs
and gnomes, who race ferociously on ahead.
As the sun begins to set magenta, peach and yellow,
the peepers grab the mic with songs of

clicks, whistles and clacks.
All of Nature has come out to play,
slowly softening and winding down
as day comes resting into night.

"The world is helpless reeling"*

in the melodrama of illusion
cleverly captivating my attention.
How to pull back the curtain,
to move beyond the superficial play of light?
I breathe deeply,
smile into the Heart,
sing praises to the Oriole bird songs,
baby birds busily fed until fledged.
Spring fills with new babies,
hope in the form of bunnies and beans,
new growth sprouts everywhere.
Days grow warmer.
Cycles of soaking rain dampen earth
encouraging life.
Moving beneath the surface,
within the soil, mycelium send out connections
linking up underground life
into immense networks of intelligence.
The energy of Earth and Sky fed by Holy Light

---

* from Hafiz, *Stay Close to those Sounds,* translated by Daniel Ladinsky in *The Gift,* 1999.

animates the visible puppet show, and
feeds the whole with so much Love.
As I open my heart,
I catch the waves flowing beyond illusion
into the sacredness of life everywhere.
The reeling becomes a stillness.
The puppets deflate.
Life streams webs of connection
through the agency of love.

CLETHRA

Summer arrives

overflowing with green energy.
The gardens offer bright flowers
each lining up for their turn at front stage.
Heart shaped juicy red strawberries are bountiful
much to the delight of the chipmunks
who leave a pile half eaten
in the center of the patch each day.
They are kind enough to save me a few.
Blueberries, blackberries, raspberries grow plump
well-watered by heavily laden clouds,
who sometime can't hold back their excitement,
but instead dump their raindrop load all at once.
Then the sun shines, clearing the sky,
making me smile
bringing all that's needed for a good garden.
Planting two pecans and two elderberries,
I watch them take root
sprouting new green shoots
that will become huge branches.
Weeding, mulching, transplanting, harvesting,
watching plants grow strong,
promising good food for the table
as fingers dig deep into the soil,
engaging my heart in a summer song of love.

I'm feeling unrooted

struggling to center
needing desperately to set down anchor
instead I'm rolling on the open sea
waves wash over the sides
sails flutter.
I'm too distracted.
I can't seem to steady the helm,
breath flows unevenly.
I will take my pipe,
sit with oak and pray.
I will breathe deeply
into Eight Brocades of QiGong.
I will go for a long slow walk forest walk
and come home to myself.
I know the cure.
The ship will right itself again.

As the sun opens

its eye to day
trees bathe themselves in color and depth.
Last night's dew, still clinging to branch tips,
flashes rainbows of light shimmering
when caught up by a gentle breeze.
Birds fill the wooded wetland
with their morning prayers
until they fade into the busyness of a new day.
Then catbird begins to orchestrate a solo,
cleverly weaving borrowed songs
into one long amazing musical piece.
I walk through my garden
gathering a mouthful of plump blueberries,
admiring pumpkin, squash and cucumber vines
flowing up fences and down the garden paths.
The first ripe cherry tomatoes bursting with flavor
are certainly no relative to the store bought kind.
A first few purple beans lay hidden under leaves,
while one lone cucumber tries
to push its way through the fence.
The day is full of gratitude
for the warmth of summer and friendships.

The sun, a fire ball of red, drops into the western sea,
as the sky turns peach shading into blue and gray.
Light fades, trees lose their depth,
silhouetted against the sky like huge stage props
waiting in the dark for the light to bring them back to life.

A Rain Dance

Standing on parched earth
Watching grey bottomed clouds pass by
Pleading
One drop, two drops
Whatever you can spare...

Remembering long ago in 1980,
a Holy day on Third Mesa,
under a crystal clear blue sky
crops of corn lay thirsty in desert heat.
Corn Maidens sprinkled a gift of corn meal
for the dry Earth.
Having spent the night in the kiva
feeding snakes corn pollen,
men began to enter in pairs
filling the central courtyard.
While one held a rattlesnake in his mouth,
his partner shook a rattle
keeping a gentle continuous rhythm.
Circling the plaza three times they came and went
dancing in a Sacred Manner.
Clouds began to gather

Lightning flashed
Thunder rolled
Rain fell,
feeding corn and the people.

No rattlesnakes live on Cape Cod
but perhaps
dancing in a Sacred Manner
would entice the clouds
to let down their sustenance.

Amazingly the rain did come!
A day of mist
moved into a night of thunder and lightning.
Gusts of wind pushed buckets of water
against the windowpane.
Gardens and ponds drank thirstily.
Soggy Earth gurgled happily.
As day broke, the deluge turned back to mist.
While frogs danced,
ponds and gardens sang oh so happily.
Gratitude flowed unceasingly for the gift of abundant rain.

The Drought

After more than a month of dry
a little rain finally
lands on dry leaves
        clacking,
cool drops slide down sweaty skin.
soundless light flashes,
the smell of warm wet asphalt rises up.
From dry lawns comes the healing scent of Sweetgrass,
        sipping thirstily.
Crickets muffle their late summer song,
not remembering what it feels like
        to be wet.
On the horizon gray clouds separate
revealing an undercoat of blue fringed with pink.
Is this wetness just a tease
        when green leaves droop
        and ponds shrink
        sharing hidden parts of themselves?

We call out:
        "Take us seriously
        brittle and brown
        shriveled and wilted,

we need help!
Bathe us in your bounty
soak our root toes in cool wetness
let us drink long lasting sighs of satisfaction
revitalizing our bodies, minds, and spirits!"

I'm conjuring up a community rain dance,
Imagining
children lining up in colorful clothes
adults join in
I'm wearing a broad-brimmed hat
with long ribbons hanging,
paper raindrops glued on it
cloud shapes surround the crown.
Everyone has a instrument
bells,
a tambourine,
a rattle,
a wand with streamers,
wind chimes,
a rain stick,
a penny whistle
jumping
turning
singing
skipping
walking, but certainly not in a straight line.
Trees sway,
leaf music abounds,
crickets saw away
creating the drone
for the insect Mariachi band.

Maybe there's a dragon
his body a long blanket
with many legs sticking out underneath
winding this way and that.
Some just watch.
Some are amazed.
One by one all join in.
Shouts of joy arise
screams of delight
Serious prayers are spoken
imploring the Cloud Angels
to let down their load
gently, easily, continuously,
feeding the people, plants, trees, insects.
Flowers smile in gratitude.

And the next day it rained!!!!

A garden poem

If I were a garden,
I would dress myself in a yellow ruffled squash blossom skirt,
lacy sky-blue hydrangea petticoats peek out from underneath.
My blouse would be stripped with native white Penstemon,
dotted with tufts of Bee Balm, black eyed Susans for buttons
Asian lilies full of fragrance would serve as sleeves,
all cinched at the waist with a belt of Beach Roses.
A sweet-smelling necklace of Lavender
and Bleeding Hearts graces my throat,
while cascading stems of scarlet Crocosmia
would be woven into my hair.
Under the magic of moonlight,
my feet bare, toes wiggling in soft earth
I would dance with the company of fireflies
the whole night through
to the persistent beat of crickets and peepers
encouraged by a gentle summer breeze.

Mid Summer

To dream or not to dream
of summer breezes,
the soft currents of tides
tug at my body.
Rocking on gentle waves,
watching green tendrils of sea grasses
reach up for the light
sway gently back and forth,
great white Egrets search for food.
A lazy kayak float.
No place to go,
Nothing to do.

Visitors move me out of daily routines
into new adventures,
zooming down the bike path,
exploring a new forest outside the neighborhood,
or paddling out on the ocean bay.
Why don't I ever take myself there,
exploring beauty beyond familiar boundaries?
I could make a pact,
a promise to continue

every week or two to do something different
maybe even a little edgy,
a little beyond the comfort zone
using mid-summer to dream up
new adventures,
expanding horizons.

Forest so dry

soft pine needles underfoot
crunch and crackle,
pond shores retreat,
baring their souls,
tell us ground water
is slowly disappearing.

It's so quiet.
Air is quiet.
Birds are quiet.
Peepers and crickets are barely audible,
as if the world is holding its breath.
There's an openness
but not to fertile ground.

I pray for rain
offer tobacco
entreat cloud angels to resuscitate
wilting plants,
trees with yellowing leaves.
Life feels on the edge.

What was a small promise,
that usually disappears,
turned into a soaking of real rain,
at first hardly sinking into dry soil.
More came
creating puddles.
Gardens were smiling.
I danced around Susan Lane
umbrella in hand,
"I'm singing in the rain
what a wonderful feeling
I'm happy again."
not caring if it was now confirmed by
neighbors "there goes that crazy lady."
I was happy
especially when even more came.

The next day the scent
of marsh
of damp forest
sweeten the air.
Dank leaves felt soft under foot.
The understory sadly wilting the day before
now perked up prettily
as if the whole forest has taken
a deep breath of relief.
The birds sing out happily
filling the air with a symphony
of connection
of joy.
The insects let loose their rhythms in the evening
sounds rising and falling

in concert with thunder and lightning,
dark clouds and more rain drops.

My body catches the rhythm.
My heart finds joy in the celebration
opening once more
to center
to ground
to deep breaths
to new possibilities.

Nature dances

as branches sway sweetly back and forth, back and forth
cooled by evening breezes, lulled into a soft lullaby of leaves.
Late summer insects create a steady hum punctuated by cricket clicks.
Nature reaches out in praise of a setting sun
costumed in flamboyant silks flowing with orange, pink and crimson.
Westward, across the bay, arms of light fling skyward
from behind a border of lacy white clouds.
The sun takes a final bow,
sinking dramatically
into a golden shimmering pathway of watery light,
as day folds into night.

Stars pop out one by one
populating the sky with intricate ancient designs.
Peace settles in this dear place,
a spit of sand stretching a bent arm's length
into the vastness of the eastern ocean.
Undulating salty waters embrace the shore,
breathing wave breaths in and out, in and out.

Trees answer, whispering soft wind songs,
while fireflies dart over a wetland
filled with sweet smelling Clethra.

A long deep peaceful sigh fills my body,
as my eyelids grow heavy.
Sleep begins to overtake consciousness,
inviting me into another dream filled world.

As seasons turn

leftover hurricane winds
tickle the trees
just as leaves begin to show
a tinge of color
making them laugh
as they dance gracefully
toes finally wet
grateful for the bounty of rain
welcoming the cool change of seasons.
I open to internal quiet,
breath deepens
my dog asleep at my feet
musical notes from wind chimes,
sing the change of the seasons
ushering in chilly air.
Trees begin to dress for fall glory.
I want to hunker down under warm blankets
take a nap
or maybe pick cranberries with a friend.
no rush
no push
opening from the inside out slowly

while the external world tumbles and turns
twisting its way
wobbling along a circuitous route
dizzying.
Like Ferdinand the bull
in the childhood story,
I want to sit under the cork tree
and watch the clouds slowly slip by,
smelling moist earth
and wait for winter's sleep.

Fall Equinox

Ba boom
Ba boom
Ba boom
Drums echo the Heartbeat of Grandmother Earth
This day of Ma'at, Truth,
Equal day/equal night.
How to bring balance when so much feels out of balance?
A world filled with pain.
Politicians playing a game of cards with Earth's future
often for their own gain,
filling their pockets jingling with gold
seeking power for power's sake.
Wake up!
We're dancing on the edge of extinction!
Time is running out quickly.
Earthly life is held in precarious balance,
Spinning, spinning
A wobbly gyroscope
Ba boom
Ba boom
Ba boom

Where does the Truth lie?
        in the beating of a smiling Heart expanding,
        in the soft touch of Wind,
        in the abundant harvest of acorns, grapes, apples
in spite of the challenges of fire, wind, water?
Noticing the continuity of Her gifts,
        of Her astounding cyclical beauty?
Slowing down to the subtle seasonal changes
        the colors,
        the smell of air and earth,
        the quality of light.
As Nature shifts, birds and butterflies flock up
into vast networks of support for long migrations.
Nighttime peepers and crickets
sing raucous lullabies of appreciation and gratitude.
I count my squash,
        collect fallen apples,
        make applesauce
        pick sweet smelling grapes
        offered up in Nature's wild garden,
        make beautiful red grape jelly
        share the bounty with friends and family.
This is the season of sorting through
like panning for gold,
dipping our sieves into the stream bed,
carefully shaking out the contents,
letting go of sand and pebbles,
looking for that one nugget of gold.
What is precious and what is not?
Unpacking winter clothes in fall's cool air,
what to keep and what to give away?

Going deeper
What sustains the moments of Truth?
What provides a balanced and harmonious life?
        treasured memories?
        this breath?
        this present moment?
        this heart opening to connect with all of Life,
        both the yin and yang of it?
Ba boom
Ba boom
Ba boom
The Heartbeat of Grandmother
sets the tone for Life in Her domain.
It's time to stop and listen
finding balance and harmony in each step,
living Ma'at with each breath...

Time on your hands?

Clean out the inside closets
of old regrets
forgiving yourself
for past indiscretions
for mistakes once made.
Toss them into boxes
take them to the dump
Make room for loving you.

What's hiding in the basement?
Cobwebs of old fears
feelings of not being enough
or being too much?
What lurks in some dark corner?
Or are treasures hidden
secreted away
waiting
for the exact right moment
to come to light?
Embrace them all
love yourself immensely.

Take courage
shine the light of love
in those dark places
extending
releasing
refreshing
meet yourself anew.
Be bold
bring forward
into this new world
someone who comes
to serve the greater good.

Magnificent Fall

Patterns of leaves dress the forest path
some edges rounded
some sharply pointed
some clusters turning red
while yellow maple leaves splattered in red
test a creative edge.
The fall costume ball begins
with gowns of delicate yellow,
muted orange, bright red and vibrant scarlet.
Each one says, "pick me,"
"oh please pick me, I'm certainly the prettiest in the forest."
Dark green pines show off these beauties
individual in shape and color
until, like the firework's finale,
the whole mountainside is aflame with color,
a multicolored quilt laid down to soften the rocky ledges.
When the rainy wind comes
the sky fills with yellow sugar maple leaves gently swirling
as trees toss confetti to the admiring crowd of birds and squirrels
filling up the forest floor with color,
laying down a patchwork quilt to keep the Mother warm
while waiting for drifts of snow
to add a white feather bed for long winter dreams.

As a Fall morning begins

clouds paint moving lacy white patterns
magnificently onto a baby blue sky.
Trees lay layers of brightly colored leaves
falling festively on wet green ground.
A waning crescent moon curves,
its light lingering a little longer
before disappearing into deep blue
as the sun fills up the world
with golden light.
This light, picked up by trees,
shines scrumptiously
illuminating leaves, a multitude of shades
of luscious lemon yellow,
ravenous red and over the top orange.
A bright bird flies to the topmost branch
to sing the world awake.

Thanksgiving as a celebration

Thanksgiving as a conflicted holiday
Memories of family feasts
celebrating bounty
celebrating family
singing "We gather together"
eating until we can eat no more
  turkey
  stuffing
  creamed onions
  butternut squash
  piles of mashed potatoes
  pumpkin pie
  mincemeat pie
  you know the drill
but if you look out the window
and through the woods
another story comes into focus.
Native Americans generous in their giving
keeping those odd-looking white people alive.
Little did they guess,
although perhaps Medicine Men and Women
scrying the future could see

nothing but heartache and devastation.
No bounty given in return,
just bounty hunters keeping them on the run,
killing rampantly "This land is our land"
freedom for everyone with white skin.
Emancipation proclamation
begins a change
only many generations later
after unimaginable damage.
It's a sad story.
When Thanksgiving is not returned
            the Earth suffers
            people suffer
only now do a few wake up
trying to make it right
trying to make a Thanksgiving for all
instead of a day of mourning.

As I focus,

a doorway opens
Nature's lifeline connects to heart light,
tendrils of energy extend outward
as my belly engages deep breaths of air.
Encouraging the mind to empty,
releasing the days debris
the body fills with free-flowing love
like ocean waves
washing over the shores of my being
creating a sense of wholeness.
Parts gather together
        with light
        with breath
        with a smile.
My self is no longer experienced as separate.
There's no differentiation,
joining as one living being.

A thought enters about anything
the day's schedule
what I need to share about the walk
what I had for breakfast.

meaningless really.
The spell immediately breaks
connection severed
Nature's door slams shut.
I mourn this transcendent loss.

Trees sated with rain.
Oaks dress in pungent orange.
Wind adding more color to the ground.
Lawns brown with summer drought
now grow vibrantly green.
It should be a time of settling in,
putting gardens to bed
completing last outdoor chores
but there's uncertainty in the air
anxiety nips at my heels.
So much feels at stake.
The future of our country.
Old ways of deep prejudice rise to the surface
as women's rights are torn away again,
some white men wanting to be in charge of everything,
enhancing wealth for wealth's sake.
Truth vs self-serving falsehoods battle.
Can we find peace again,
a place for the common good,
cooperation for the benefit of all?

The sun is warm.
The trees are radiant.
Seagulls dance playfully on the waves in the bay.
The tides, as always, move in and out.
The moon grows full and thins again.

Seasons continued despite human disruption.

Later, I walk around Susan Lane.
It's dark.
The sky is clear, filled to the brim with stars,
opening the door to transcendent mystery.
I fill with the clarity of night
knowing this human soap opera will play itself out.
Breathing deeply,
Shoulders drop.
Feet soften.
My heart opens to dance the soft shoe
of glory to all of creation.
No matter what,
life goes on with choices of how we live it.

The Power of the Heart

What if there was an immense power
held in every leaf
in every blade of grass
in the breath of a baby
in every strand of your hair
in every ray of sunlight?

What would you do if that power emanated
from inside of you
and your neighbor
and your enemy?

What if that power was so beautiful,
filling you with the grace and love
of Christ
of Buddha
of Allah
of the Tao
of the Creator?

How would you sit with it?
How would you use it?

What would you do with it?
Where would you take it?
Could you simply be with it, hold it?

Open your heart!
Release the floodgates!
Let the Light move
into every nook and cranny or your being!
Sing from the top of the mountain!
Dance in the river valleys!
Let joy fill you to the brim!

Grace and Divine Love are yours
        to bath in
        to be in
        to share with yourself, your family
        with your neighbor
        with your enemy
        your community near and global
        with your Earth community
        and All of Life Everywhere.
No holds barred, there's an infinite supply to go around!

Like Hafiz

I want to cover you with Holy Light,
letting words tumble down from the Heavens
born on the waves of sunlight
and the wings of Angels.
Feel the warmth of their wings flutter around you,
fanning love into your heart,
let the brightness of sunlight
enter through the pores of your skin,
lifting you into ecstasy and grace.
Bathe in the presence of trees,
in the sweet wetness of a summer shower
or the coolness of a fall breeze
or the taste of a snowflake on your tongue.
Connect into the vast web of life
dancing with confidence and joy
within this vast community we call home.

At the close

of day
when the busyness of the world begins to settle,
I walk slowly down the forest path
soft with sand and pine underfoot,
air permeated with the scent of forest life.
A breeze moves through leaves and branches
singing a coming into night lullaby,
accompanied by the settling sounds of birds,
by the rhythms of crickets and peepers,
murmuring evening songs of connection.
The distant sounds of waves along the sandy shore
provides comforting continuity
while letting go of day.
Extending my energy into this sea of aliveness,
recognizing the threads of life
woven into a massive Earthly quilt,
a broad smile spreads across my face.
I come home to peace
without judgement,
accepting life as it is with a full Heart.

Carol Marcy

As a child... *

I roamed the hills
        collecting cows teeth and freedom.
From the flooded farm fields below,
        I brought home frogs
        filling the window wells with life.
In the barn across the street,
        sandpaper tongues sucked my fingers
        liquid brown Jersey eyes reflected mine.
Behind the field behind the barn,
        I set sail on winter ice ponds
        skating, twirling, dancing to the tune
        of thunderous notes of cracking ice.
Up in the tree behind the house,
        I swayed with the wind
        forever
        out of sight out of mind.
Adventures down woodland trails
        brought courage, daring, strength and skill.
I wanted to be a farmer not a housewife

* Inspired by the poems of Joy Harjo

to be someone with agency like my father
not stuck behind a typewriter.
Was I born into the wrong body or adopted
or living on the wrong side of history?
Whose ghost was chasing me away from home?

I am of the generation when my mother opened the door and said, "Be home for lunch." I had tremendous freedom to explore the natural world around me. Later, she supported my interest in Girl Scouts, sometimes driving me to camp in another state. There I learned outdoor living skills and had opportunities to hike and appreciate forest life. I distinctly remember hiking down a woodland ravine, hearing the Wood Thrush sing and saying to myself that someday I wanted to own property where there were Wood Thrush. That's inadvertently happened twice.

As an adult, my husband and I bought land in Northern Vermont as a summer getaway from the heat of New York City. We built a log cabin from scratch, beginning with cutting the logs and peeling the bark. We eventually moved there to homestead. We had running water but no electricity, which became a way to tune in more deeply with the cycles of nature. I had a huge garden from which I fed our family. Our second son was born in that house.

Much later, I became involved with the Washington Center for Consciousness Studies. For many years I attended a weekly seminar and deepened my meditation practice. I also worked as a psychologist in Southern Maryland, living in the woods, taking clients on walks when it was appropriate and leading woodland retreats. I became involved in a Native American sweat lodge community.

These are some of the roots that have fostered my abiding love for Forest Bathing Walks.

www.ingramcontent.com/pod-product-compliance
Lightning Source LLC
Chambersburg PA
CBHW071446090426
42737CB00011B/1801

* 9 7 9 8 2 1 8 9 6 6 7 9 9 *